GENE PERRET

GRANDchildren are So Much Fun WE SHOULD HAVE Had Them First

COVER ILLUSTRATION BY
GARY LOCKE

WitWorks™
a funny little division of arizona highways books

2039 West Lewis Avenue, Phoenix, Arizona 85009
Telephone: (602) 712-2200
Web site: www.witworksbooks.com

Publisher — Win Holden
Managing Editor — Bob Albano
Associate Editor — Evelyn Howell
Associate Editor — P. K. McMahon
Art Director — Mary Winkelman Velgos
Photography Director — Peter Ensenberger
Production Director — Cindy Mackey

Library of Congress Catalog Number 00-111063
ISBN 1893860612

GRANDCHILDREN ARE SO MUCH FUN WE SHOULD HAVE HAD THEM FIRST
FIRST EDITION, published in 2001.
Printed in the United States.

Book designer — Mary Winkelman Velgos

There is such a thing as
second childhood. It's called
"being a grandparent."

If we play it right, we can get
through grandparenthood without
ever changing a diaper.

But don't forget — grandparenting
requires training. If you never had
children, you probably shouldn't
have grandchildren.

"Someday you'll have
children of your own"
is a threat. "Someday you'll have
grandchildren of your own"
is a blessing.

Still, it's more fun
to love someone
when you don't have to pay
for their college education.

GRANDCHILDREN ARE

SO LOVABLE — UNTIL

THE DAY THEY

OUTDRIVE YOU ON

THE GOLF COURSE.

"Hiya, Pop-pop" is probably

the second most

welcome phrase in

the entire world.

The most welcome is

"Bye-bye, Pop-pop."

It's always easy to make

your grandchildren laugh.

Show them your

wedding pictures.

MY GRANDDAUGHTER AND I

ARE INSEPARABLE.

SHE KEEPS ME

WRAPPED AROUND

HER LITTLE FINGER.

I'm a firm

disciplinarian

with my

granddaughter.

Yessir, I've got her

exactly

where she wants me.

My children used to call
when they needed money.

Now they call
when they need
a baby-sitter.

It's always a delight

to have the

grandchildren

visit.

The operative word here

is "visit."

There are two
things that I tell my
grandchildren repeatedly:
"Pop-pop loves you,"
and "Pop-pop
needs a rest now."

Retirement and grandparenthood

go hand in hand.

Once the grandkids

leave for the day, you don't

want to get up the next morning

and have to go to work.

As a grandparent I feel

a responsibility to go to all

the Little League games:

To watch my grandson play,

and to make sure

my daughter behaves

herself in the stands.

It's quite easy to
grow old gracefully — unless
you have grandchildren.

Then you grow old
at whatever pace
they set for you.

There's only one
cutest grandchild in the whole
world — every grandparent has
a picture of it.

So, grandparents can say,
"Be nice to me or
I'll start showing you pictures
of my grandchildren."

NOTHING

AGES YOU FASTER

THAN A GRANDCHILD

WITH A

DRIVER'S LICENSE.

There are some days

when all I want is

to see my grandchildren

. . . go home.

Children will

always

act like children.

Grandparents will often

act like accomplices.

Spoiling

the grandkids and

then sending them home

is a little like picking

wild mushrooms

for someone else

to eat.

When they behave,

they're my grandchildren.

When they misbehave,

they're my

daughter's kids.

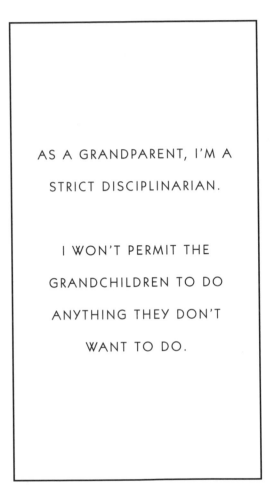

AS A GRANDPARENT, I'M A
STRICT DISCIPLINARIAN.

I WON'T PERMIT THE
GRANDCHILDREN TO DO
ANYTHING THEY DON'T
WANT TO DO.

I always give

my grandkids

a couple of quarters

when they go home.

It's a bargain.

Children are a joy forever.

Grandchildren

are a joy

until about

4 o'clock

in the afternoon.

My grandkids and I share

a common bond:

I've either forgotten or

don't care anymore about

things they haven't learned yet.

AS GRANDCHILDREN GROW

OLDER AND MORE MATURE,

YOU CAN WATCH

THEIR LOVE FOR YOU

TURN TO TOLERANCE.

Being human,

i sometimes lose patience

with my grandchild.

An example would be

during our trip to Disneyland

when I said, "Hey, how

about letting me ride

in that stroller for awhile?"

Two things

I dislike about my

granddaughter — when

she won't take her afternoon

nap, and when

she won't let me

take mine.

Grandchildren don't

stay young forever,

which is good

because Pop-pops

have only so many

horsey rides in them.

There's a

brief period

between when your children

mature and when they produce

grandchildren.

Use that time to

finally display your precious

knickknacks safely.

I ALWAYS INTENDED

TO GROW OLD GRACEFULLY.

I JUST SEEM TO BE

DOING IT FASTER

SINCE THE

GRANDCHILDREN

ARRIVED.

I don't intentionally
spoil my grandkids.

It's just that
correcting them
often takes more energy
than I have left.

My granddaughter
gets irritable when
she has to take her
midday nap, and
I get irritable
when I don't.

I LIKE TO DO NICE THINGS

FOR MY GRANDCHILDREN —

LIKE BUY THEM THOSE TOYS

I'VE ALWAYS WANTED

TO PLAY WITH.

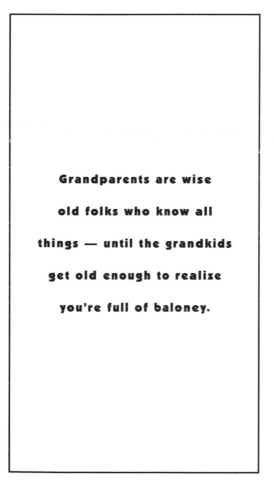

Grandparents are wise
old folks who know all
things — until the grandkids
get old enough to realize
you're full of baloney.

Everyone

should have

grandchildren.

It's not fun going

through your

second childhood

alone.

Grandparenting is fun.

You can do things with

your grandchildren

you never allowed

your own kids to do.

IT'S AMAZING HOW

GRANDPARENTS SEEM

SO YOUNG

ONCE YOU BECOME ONE.

Why are

all grandchildren

so adorable and cute?

In my case,

I think it's

good breeding.

Kids love Mom-mom and

Pop-pop's house

for the same reason

cowboys loved the Old West:

It's a place where seldom

is heard a discouraging word

. . . and when the grandkids

leave, it looks like a home

where the buffalo roamed.

MY MEMORY MUST

BE FAILING.

I CAN'T REMEMBER

EVER HAVING

AS MUCH ENERGY

AS MY GRANDKIDS.

A grandchild is

a perfect bundle of joy.

That's because when

they cease to be a joy,

you hand them

back to their parents.

Having a grandchild is great.

It's all of the joy

and none of

the hospital bills.

THE GREATEST TOY

I'VE EVER HAD

TO PLAY WITH

WAS A GRANDCHILD.

Grandparenting

is a joy forever

because even though

the grandchildren

grow and mature,

the grandparents

don't have to.

Becoming a grandparent

is a revelation.

I never thought

I could be

so fond of

someone else's kid.

My children
used to tell me how much
they loved me just
because I was their mommy.

Now that I'm a grandparent,
my children tell me
how much they love me
just because
I'm their baby-sitter.

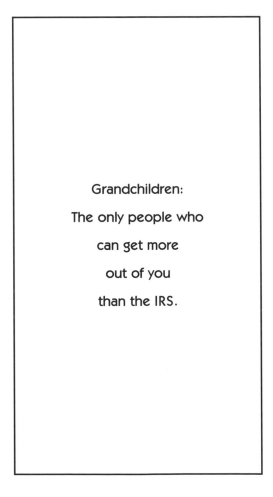

Grandchildren:

The only people who

can get more

out of you

than the IRS.

Grandpop is someone who

occasionally keeps an

eye on the baby.

Grandmom is someone who

occasionally keeps an

eye on the baby

and Grandpop.

As a grandfather

I sometimes get annoyed

at my young grandson.

It's called "sibling rivalry."

I have a lot

in common with

my granddaughter.

For one thing,

we're both

the same age.

I love to play "hide and go seek"

with my granddaughter.

Although some days

my goal is to find

a hiding place

where she can't find me

until after high school.

Sometimes

my granddaughter

can be very stubborn.

For instance,

she refuses to believe

that's really me

in my wedding pictures.

My grandchild has taught me
what true love means.

It means watching
Scooby-Doo cartoons
while the basketball game
is on another channel.

Grandparenting requires patience.

That means going to a 3-year-old's

ballet recital and sitting quietly

while the non-talented

children perform.

Grandchildren would be

more fun if they were

the same age as we are.

(And the kids feel

the same way about us.)

PLAYING WITH

THE GRANDKIDS

CAN MAKE YOU

FEEL YOUNG AT HEART

AND OLD

OF BODY.

Playing with

my grandchildren

brings out the kid in me.

It also brings out

the liniment

after they leave.

Often, there's tension

between my grandchildren

and me because of the

difference in age.

They're so much more

mature than I am.

GRANDPARENTS

ARE SWEET AND WISE

OLD FOLKS

WHO NEVER BUY A KID

CLOTHES FOR A

BIRTHDAY PRESENT.

Sure I spoil my grandkids.

Every child should

have something

he or she doesn't need —

like grandparents.

To be a grandparent

you must be old enough

to be able to act

like a child.

Children

like grandparents

because even though

they're grownups,

they don't take it

too seriously.

A grandchild

is a bundle

from heaven . . .

and you don't even have

to pay any of

the shipping costs.

SURE I'VE SPOILED

MY GRANDCHILDREN,

BUT THEY NEVER

GAVE ME

A CHOICE.

When they were young,

I thought my grandchildren

were cute.

Now we've all grown older,

and they think I'm cute.

Children understand

"Mommy" and "Daddy,"

but they're not sure

exactly what grandparents are.

But they do understand

they can milk'em

for all they're worth.

IT'S NICE TO BUY TOYS FOR

THE GRANDKIDS.

IT'S A CHANCE TO BUY

SOMETHING FOR THEM

YOU WOULD NEVER BUY

FOR YOURSELF.

I tried to tell

the grandkids

I was worn out

in terms they

would understand.

I said,

"With Pop-pop,

batteries

are not included."

Mother Nature

is wonderful.

Grandchildren get

"too old"

for piggy-back rides

just about the same time

they get too heavy

for them.

MY FIRST GRANDCHILD
TAUGHT ME A LOT — LIKE
THE WORDS "POP-POP"
AND "PUSHOVER" ARE
INTERCHANGEABLE.

Bank on it — once
my grandkids are
grown and educated,
I'll never watch another
kiddie cartoon show
as long as I live.

A GRANDCHILD IS A

BLACKMAILER

WITH THE SMILE

OF AN ANGEL.

Being a grandparent

has fulfilled

a lifelong

dream of mine.

I've often said,

"When I grow up,

I want to be a child."

When I was a child,

my mother wouldn't let me

misbehave.

When I was a parent, I

wouldn't let the children

misbehave.

Now I'm a grandparent — **watch out!**

There's no such thing
as a "bad" child.

Only a "good" child
doing things
that his grandfather
egged him on to do.

My grandson wears me out.

By the time he leaves,
I look like the picture
he drew of me
in pre-school.

Sure we spoil

our grandchildren.

It's what happens when

an irresistible force

meets an object that's

too doggone worn out

to be immovable.

True love is reading

a children's book aloud

to your 3-year old grandchild

while there are other adults

in the room.

GRANDMOM IS

THE LAST WORD

IN BABY-SITTING.

GRANDPOP IS THE

LAST RESORT.

Children learn

early that

"Pop-pop said it's OK"

doesn't mean

it's OK.

"You're more trouble

than the children are"

is the

greatest compliment

a grandparent

can receive.

GRANDPARENTS

ARE THERE

TO HELP THE CHILD

GET INTO MISCHIEF

THEY HAVEN'T

THOUGHT OF YET.

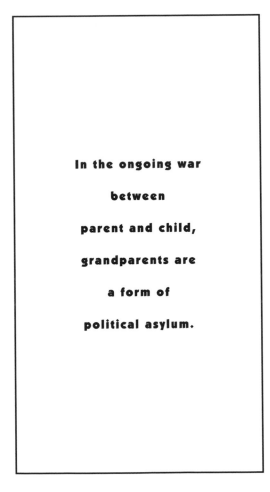

In the ongoing war

between

parent and child,

grandparents are

a form of

political asylum.

I roll around on the floor

with my grandchildren

the same as

I used to do

with my own kids.

But with the grandkids,

it takes longer

to get up.

Ending of
a child's night prayer:
" . . . and make me a
good boy — oh,
never mind.
I don't have
to be good tomorrow.
We're going to
Grandmom's."

I make it a point to

teach my young granddaughter

that she can't always have

whatever she wants — then

I give it to her.

If God didn't want us

to spoil our grandchildren,

why'd He make them

so cute?

HOW COME MY

GRANDDAUGHTER ALWAYS

HAS HER WAY WITH ME

EVEN THOUGH

I HAVE SENIORITY?

WITH GRANDCHILDREN,
YOU JUST LOVE THEM
AND LET SOMEBODY
ELSE RAISE THEM.

Grandchildren

are the

fringe benefits of

raising a family.

Grandpops are
Nature's way of saying,
"I don't care if you
are tired and aging,
you're still
going to give
horsey rides."

Playing with

the grandchildren

can be exhausting,

but it's usually easier

than trying to

say "no."

You can usually get

whatever you want

by being hardworking,

dedicated, and persevering — or

by being 4 years old

and asking

one of your grandparents.

MY GRANDDAUGHTER PLAYS

"HIDE AND GO SEEK"

WITH MY WIFE.

WITH ME, SHE PLAYS

"HIDE AND GO WAKE

UP GRANDPOP."

Grandchildren
and grandparents make good
strategic allies.

They have the parents
surrounded by age.

Mother Nature is wonderful.

My granddaughter arrived

just when my hair

was leaving.

A GRANDDAUGHTER

IS SUGAR AND SPICE

AND EVERYTHING

NICE — ESPECIALLY

WHEN SHE'S

TAKING A NAP.

Grandparents and grandchildren

can both get grouchy at times.

The difference is that

the children

usually have

a logical reason for it.

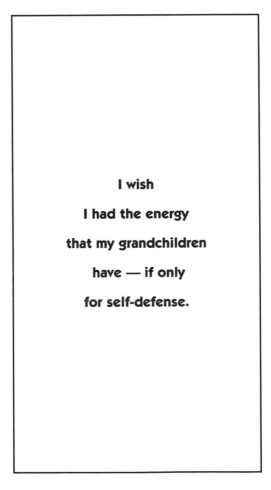

I wish

I had the energy

that my grandchildren

have — if only

for self-defense.

What a bargain

grandchildren are!

I give them my loose change,

and they give me a million dollars'

worth of pleasure.

My grandson expects a monetary reward when he behaves for me.

He says, "Pop-pop, you wouldn't want me to be good for nothing, would you?"

My granddaughter wants to

marry me when she grows up.

She'll change her mind

when she realizes

I'll be out of quarters

by then.

MY 4-YEAR-OLD
GRANDDAUGHTER
ALREADY KNOWS
RIGHT FROM WRONG.

SHE'S ALWAYS
RIGHT,
AND I'M ALWAYS
WRONG.

Grandparents

may not make

the best baby-sitters

in the world,

but you can't beat

the prices.

Grandparents

should be allowed to spoil

their grandchildren.

For some of us,

it's the only fun we can have

without getting

our doctor's permission.

Granddaughters are

the cutest thing in the world,

and grandpops

are the sweetest thing

in the world — provided

they've both

had their naps.

GRANDCHILDREN ARE

A LUXURY

YOU CAN STILL AFFORD

ON A

FIXED INCOME.

What is a grandfather?

It's the answer to the

angry question,

"Who taught you that?"

Our grandkids always run to

Grandmom when they

get in trouble.

It confuses the parents.

As my daughter says, "If I had

done what she did, I would have

run away from you."

(And Grandmom adds, "And I

would have chased you, too.")

I always answer

every question my

grandchildren ask.

They'll have plenty of time

later on to learn

the correct version.

My grandchildren

never know whether

I'm telling them the truth

or feeding them

a tall story — and many times,

neither do I.

My grandkids believe

I'm the oldest thing in the world.

And after

two or three hours

with them,

I believe it, too.

There's a reason why
grandparents always give in
to their grandchildren.

It's much safer than
trying to
outsmart them.

Never show your

grandchildren your

class photo

from high school.

They may ask,

"Which one is you?"

If you want to continue

to grow old

peacefully and gracefully,

never let your grandchildren

learn the word

"Why."

TRY NEVER TO CUSS

AROUND YOUR

GRANDCHILDREN.

LET SOMEONE ELSE

DRIVE.

Always throw a diaper over
your shoulder when holding
your new grandchild.

Because you know what
they say — "Out of the
mouths of babes . . ."

GRANDPOPS ARE

GOOD WITH KIDS.

WE CAN OUT-CRANKY THEM.

Grandkids always run

to their grandmom when

they're in trouble.

Come to think of it,

so do grandpops.

Granddaughter: "Are

you sure this

is a cartoon show,

Pop-pop?"

Pop-pop: "Yes,

I am, Honey.

Now be quiet

so Pop-pop

can hear the score."

Do you know why

grandchildren

are always

so full of energy?

They suck it out of

their grandparents.

When my grandson

misbehaved,

I said, "I can still put you

over my knee."

He said, "The good one

or the bad one?"

Between

grandparents and

grandchildren

there's a huge

difference in age,

but a striking

similarity

in mentality.

Grandparents are

easy to find.

They're wrapped around

their grandchild's

little finger.

Grandpops and grandchildren

get along well together.

They share the same

likes, dislikes,

and nap times.

When grandchildren

are in trouble,

they run to Grandmom.

They would run to Grandpop,

but he's generally the one

who got them into trouble

in the first place.

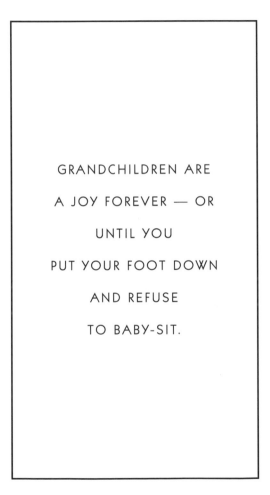

GRANDCHILDREN ARE

A JOY FOREVER — OR

UNTIL YOU

PUT YOUR FOOT DOWN

AND REFUSE

TO BABY-SIT.

As a grandparent

I learned why

they call them

the "Terrible Two's."

At about that age,

they start

beating you regularly

in the "Candyland Game."

ON THE SEVENTH DAY

GOD RESTED.

HIS GRANDCHILDREN

MUST HAVE BEEN

OUT OF TOWN.

Grandparents are
wise old folks — wise enough
to know they're being
outsmarted by
a 2-year-old.

GRANDPARENTS

DON'T

GROW OLD — THEY

CAME THAT WAY.

Grandchildren are here

to break

all the keepsakes

that survived your

own children.

An hour

with your grandchildren

can make you

feel young again.

Anything longer than that,

and you start to age quickly.

Children are so gullible.

They believe everything their

grandfather tells them.

Or is Grandpop gullible

because he thinks the kids are

actually buying this stuff?

They say children

should be seen

and not heard.

Sometimes the way

Grandpop dresses,

he shouldn't even

be seen.

Grandchildren

are sent

to help us grandparents

grow younger

gracefully.

Children are young

for only a little while.

Grandparents are

young forever.

PARENTS

PROCEED WITH

CAUTION — GRANDPARENTS

AT WORK.

Grandchildren

are active;

grandparents are spry.

Active always wins.

I have a warm feeling

after playing with

my grandchildren.

It's the

liniment working.

GRANDPARENTING'S

ONE JOB

WHERE SENIORITY

MEANS ABSOLUTELY

NOTHING.

Grandparents

should be a

good example to their

grandchildren — that

you never have

to grow up.

Other Funny Little Books From **WitWorks**

**Cow Pie Ain't No Dish
You Take to the County Fair**
Cartoonist Jim Willoughby
and a team of writers churn
up fun with their version of
cowboys' facts of life.
$6.95   #ACWP7

**Never Give a Heifer
a Bum Steer**
Arizona's official historian
Marshall Trimble bases his
jokes and tall tales on the folks
he grew up with in Ash Fork.
$7.95   #ANVP9

**Growing Older is
So Much Fun
EVERYBODY'S Doing It**
Gene Perret delivers a spate of
one-liners that cast a funny
glow over senior citizenship.
$6.95   #AGOP0

**Someday I Want to Go
to All the Places
My Luggage Has Been**
Gene Perret's brief essays
poke fun at the things about
travel that bug us.
$7.95   #ALLP9

**Never Stand Between a
Cowboy and His Spittoon**
Here's a gross of jokes taken
from newspapers published
before Arizona became a state
in 1912. Some are classy.
Others are crass. But all are a
historical reflection of what
was funny at the time.
$6.95   #ABLP0

Do You Pray, Duke?
Cowboy-oriented chuckles
from cartoonist Jim
Willoughby.
$6.95   #ADDP0

**Retirement:
Twice the Time,
Half the Money**
A few months after retire-
ment, the humor sets in: You
have a lot of time on your
hands but less money in your
wallet. What does that mean?
Emmy-winning humor writer
Gene Perret has the answers.
$6.95   #ARTS2

*available
in bookstores*

To order a book or request a catalog from WitWorks™
call toll-free **1-800-543-5432**.
In Phoenix or outside the U.S., call **602-712-2000**.
Online at **www.witworksbooks.com**